The Gododdin Poems

William F. Skene

The Gododdin Poems

Table of Contents

Table of Contents

The Gododdin Poems

The Gododdin Poems

Table of Contents

The Gododdin Poems

The Gododdin Poems

William F. Skene

Kessinger Publishing reprints thousands of hard–to–find books!

Visit us at http://www.kessinger.net

The Gododdin Poems

The Goddoddin Poems

The Gododdin Poems

ANEURIN

from *The Four Ancient Books of Wales*

by William F. Skene

[1869]

This is the 'Gododdin'. Aneurin composed it.

I

Of manly disposition was the youth,
Valour had he in the tumult;
Fleet thick−maned chargers
Were under the thigh of the illustrious youth;
A shield, light and broad,
Was on the slender swift flank,
A sword, blue and bright,
Golden spurs, and ermine.
It is not by me
That hatred shall be shown to thee;
I will do better towards thee,
To celebrate thee in poetic eulogy.
Sooner hadst thou gone to the bloody bier
Than to the nuptial feast;
Sooner hadst thou gone to be food for ravens
Than to the conflict of spears;
Thou beloved friend of Owain!
Wrong it is that he should be under ravens.
It is evident in what region
The only son of Marro was killed.

The Gododdin Poems

II

Caeawg, the leader, wherever he came,
Breathless in the presence of a maid would he distribute the mead;
The front of his shield was pierced, when he heard
The shout of battle, he would give no quarter wherever he pursued;
He would not retreat from the combat, until he caused
Blood to stream; like rushes would he hew down the men who would
not yield.
The Gododdin does not relate, in the land of Mordai,
Before the tents of Madawg, when he returned,
Of but one man in a hundred that came back.

III

Caeawg, the combatant, the stay of his country,
Whose attack is like the rush of the eagle into the sea, when allured by
his prey;
He formed a compact, his signal was observed;
Better was his resolution performed: he retreated not
Before the host of Gododdin, at the close of day.
With confidence he pressed upon the conflict of Manawyd;
And regarded neither spear nor shield.
There is not to be found a habitation that abounded in dainties,
That has been kept from the attack of the warriors.

IV

Caeawg, the leader, the wolf of the strand,
Amber wreaths encircled his brow;
Precious was the amber, worth wine from the horn.
He repelled the violence of ignoble men, and blood trickled down;
For Gwynedd and the North would have come to his share,
By the advice of the son of Ysgyrran,
Who wore the broken shield.

V

Caeawg, the leader, armed was he in the noisy conflict;
His was the foremost part of the advanced division, in front of the hosts.
Before his blades fell five battalions.
Of the men of Deivyr and Brenneich, uttering groans:
Twenty hundred perished in one hour.
Sooner did his flesh go to the wolf, than he to the nuptial feast;
He sooner became food for the raven, than approached the altar;
Before he entered the conflict of spears, his blood streamed to the ground.
It was the price of mead in the hall, amidst the throng.
Hyveidd Hir shall be celebrated as long as there will be a minstrel.

VI

The men went to Gododdin with laughter and sprightliness,
Bitter were they in the battle, displaying their blades;
A short year they remained in peace.
The son of Bodgad, by the energy of his hand, caused a throbbing.
Though they went to churches to do penance,
The old, and the young, and the bold–handed,
The inevitable strife of death was to pierce them.

VII

The men went to Gododdin, laughing as they moved:
A gloomy disaster befell their army;
Thou slayest them with blades, without much noise:
Thou, powerful pillar of living right, causest stillness.

VIII

The men went to Catraeth, loquacious was their host;
Fresh mead was their feast, and also their poison.
Three hundred were contending with weapons;

And after sportive mirth, stillness ensued!
Though they went to churches to do penance,
The inevitable strife of death was to pierce them.

IX

The men went to Catraeth, fed with mead, and drunk.
Firm and vigorous; it were wrong if I neglected to praise them.
Around the red, mighty, and murky blades
Obstinately and fiercely fought the dogs of war.
If I had judged you to be on the side of the tribe of Brenneich,
Not the phantom of a man would I have left alive.
A friend I have lost, myself being unhurt;
He openly opposed the terrible chief—
The magnanimous hero did not seek the dowry of his father−in−law;
The son of Cian of Maen Gwyngwn.

X

The men went to Catraeth with the dawn;
They dealt peaceably with those who feared them.
A hundred thousand and three hundred engaged in mutual overthrow.
Drenched in gore they served as butts for lances;
Their post they most manfully defended
Before the retinue of Mynyddawg Mwynvawr.

XI

The men went to Catraeth with the dawn;
Regretted are their absence and their disposition;
Mead they drank, yellow, sweet, ensnaring.
In that year many a minstrel fell.
Redder were their swords than their plumes.
Their blades were white as lime, their helmets split into four parts,
Before the retinue of Mynyddawg Mwynvawr.

XII

The men went to Catraeth with the day:
Have not the best of battles their disgrace?
They made biers a matter of necessity.
With blades full of vigour in defence of Baptism.
This is best before the alliance of kindred.
Exceedingly great was the bloodshed and death, of which they were the cause,
Before the army of Gododdin, when the day occurred.
Is not a double quantity of discretion the best strengthener of a hero?

XIII

The man went to Catraeth with the day:
Truly he quaffed the foaming mead on serene nights;
He was unlucky, though proverbially fortunate:
His mission, through ambition, was that of a destroyer.
There hastened not to Catraeth
A chief so magnificent
As to his design on the standard.
Never was there such a host
From the fort of Eiddyn,
That would scatter abroad the mounted ravagers.
Tudvwlch Hir, near his land and towns,
Slaughtered the Saxons for seven days.
His valour remained until he was overpowered;
And his memory will remain among his fair associates.
When Tudvwlch, the supporter of the land, arrived,
The station of the son of Cilydd became a plain of blood.

XIV

The man went to Catraeth with the dawn;
To them were their shields a protection.
Blood they sought, the gleamers assembled:

Simultaneously, like thunder, arose the din of shields.
The man of envy, the deserter, and the base,
He would tear and pierce with pikes.
From an elevated position, he slew, with a blade,
In iron affliction, a steel–clad commander;
He subdued in Mordai those that owed him homage;
Before Erthgi armies groaned.

XV

Of the battle of Catraeth, when it shall be related,
The people will utter sighs; long has been their sorrow.
There will be a dominion without a sovereign, and a murky land.
The sons of Godebawg, an upright clan,
Bore, streaming, long biers.
Sad was the fate, just the necessity,
Decreed to Tudvwlch and Cyvwlch Hir.
Together they drank the clear mead
By the light of the rushes,
Though pleasant to the taste, its banefulness lasted long.

XVI

Before Echeching, the splendid Caer, he shouted:
Young and forward men followed him;
Before, on the Bludwe the horn was poured out
In the joyful Mordai;
Before, his drink would be bragget;
Before, gold and rich purple he would display;
Before, high–fed horses would bear him safe away;
Gwrthlev and he, when he poured out the liquor,
Before, he would raise the shout, and there would be a profitable diminution;
He was a bear in his march, always unwilling to skulk.

XVII

And now the early leader,
The sun is ascending,
The sovereign from which emanates universal light.
In the heaven of the Isle of Prydain.
Direful was the flight before the shaking
Of the shield in the direction of the victor;
Bright was the horn
In the hall of Eiddyn;
With pomp was he invited
To the feast of the intoxicating mead;
He drank the beverage of wine
At the meeting of the reapers;
He drank transparent wine,
With a daring purpose.
The reapers sing of war,
War with the shining wing;
The minstrels sang of war,
Of harnessed war,
Of winged war.
No shield was unexpanded
In the conflict of spears;
Of equal eye they fell
In the struggle of battle.
Unshaken in the tumult,
Without dishonour did he retaliate;
His will had to be conciliated
Ere became a green sward
The grave of Gwrvelling the great.

XVIII

Qualities they will honour.
Three forward (chiefs or bands) of Novant,

A battalion of five hundred;
Three chiefs and three hundred;
There are three Knights of battle.
From Eiddyn, arrayed in golden armour,
Three loricated hosts.
Three Kings wearing the golden torques;
Three bold Knights.
Three equal battles;
Three of the same order, mutually jealous.
Bitterly would they chase the foe;
Three dreadful in the conflict;
Lions, that would kill dead as lead.
There was in the war a collection of gold;
Three sovereigns of the people.
Came from the Brython,
Cynri and Cenon
And Cynrain from Aeron,
To greet with ashen lances.
The Deivyr distillers.
Came there from the Brython,
A better man than Cynon,
A serpent to his sullen foes?

XIX

I drank mead and wine in Mordai,
Great was the quantity of spears
In the assembly of the warriors.
He prepared food for the eagle.
When Cydywal sallied forth, he raised
The shout with the green dawn, and dealt out tribulation;
Splintered shields about the ground he left,
With darts of awful tearing did he hew down;
In the battle, the foremost in the van
The son of Syvno wounded; the astronomer knew it.

He who sold his life,
In the face of warning,
With sharpened blades committed slaughter;
But he himself was slain by crosses and spears.
According to the compact, he meditated an attack,
And admired a pile of carcases
Of gallant men of toil,
Whom in the upper part of Gwynedd he pierced.

XX

I drank wine and mead in Mordai,
And because I drank, I fell by the side of the rampart; the fate of allurement.
Colwedd the brave was not without ambition.
When all fell, thou didst also fall.
Thus, when the issue comes, it were well if thou hadst not sinned.
Present, it was related, was a person of a daring arm.

XXI

The men went to Catraeth; they were renowned;
Wine and mead from golden cups was their beverage;
That year was to them of exalted solemnity;
Three warriors and three score and three hundred, wearing the golden torques.
Of those who hurried forth after the excess of revelling,
But three escaped by the prowess of the gashing sword,
The two war–dogs of Aeron, and Cenon the dauntless,
And myself from the spilling of my blood, the reward of my sacred song.

XXII

My friend in real distress, we should have been by none disturbed,
Had not the white Commander led forth (his army):
We should not have been separated in the hall from the banquet of mead,
Had he not laid waste our convenient position.

He who is base in the field, is base on the hearth.
Truly the Gododdin relates that after the gashing assault,
There was none more ardent than Llivieu.

XXIII

Scattered, broken, of motionless form, is the weapon,
To which it was highly congenial to prostrate the horde of the Lloegrians.
Shields were strewn in the entrance, shields in the battle of lances;
He reduced men to ashes,
And made women widows,
Before his death.
Graid, the son of Hoewgi,
With spears,
He caused the effusion of blood.

XXIV

Adan was the hero of the two shields
Whose front was variegated, and motion like that of a war–steed.
There was tumult in the mount of slaughter, there was fire,
Impetuous were the lances, there was sunshine,
There was food for ravens, for the raven there was profit.
And before he would let them go free,
With the morning dew, like the eagle in his pleasant course,
He scattered them on either side as they advanced forward.
The Bards of the world will pronounce an opinion on men of valour.
No ransom would avail those whom his standard pursued.
The spears in the hands of the warriors were causing devastation.
And ere was interred under his horses,
One who had been energetic in his commands,
His blood had thoroughly washed his armour:
Buddvan, the son of Bleiddvan the Bold.

XXV

It were wrong to leave him without a memorial, a great wrong.
He would not leave an open gap through cowardice;
The benefit of the minstrels of Prydain never quitted his court.
On the calends of January, according to his design.
His land was not ploughed, since it lay waste.
He was a mighty dragon of indignant disposition,
A commander in the bloody field after the banquet of wine;—
Gwenabwy, the son of Gwen, of the strife of Catraeth.

XXVI

True it was, as songs relate,
No one's steed overtook Marchleu.
The lances of the commander
From his prancing horse, strewed a thick path.
As he was reared to bring slaughter and support.
Furious was the stroke of his protecting sword;
Ashen shafts were scattered from the grasp of his hand.
From the stony pile;
He delighted to spread destruction.
He would slaughter with a variegated sword from a furze–bush;
As when a company of reapers comes in the interval of fine weather,
Would Marchleu cause the blood to flow.

XXVII

Issac was sent from the southern region;
His conduct resembled the flowing sea;
He was full of modesty and gentleness,
When he delightfully drank the mead.
But along the rampart of Offer to the point of Maddeu,
He was not fierce without heroism, nor did he attempt scattering without effecting it,
His sword resounded in the mouths of mothers;

He was an ardent spirit, praise be to him, the son of Gwyddneu.

XXVIII

Ceredig, lovely is his fame;
He would gain distinction, and preserve it;
Gentle, lowly, calm, before the day arrived
In which he learned the achievements of the brave:
May it be the lot of the friend of songs to arrive
In the country of heaven, and recognize his home!

XXIX

Ceredig, amiable leader,
A wrestler in the impetuous fight;
His gold–bespangled shield was conspicuous on the battle–field,
His lances were broken, and shattered into splinters,
The stroke of his sword was fierce and penetrating;
Like a man would he maintain his post.
Before he received the affliction of earth, before the fatal blow.
He had fulfilled his in guarding his station.
May he find a complete reception
With the Trinity in perfect unity.

XXX

When Caradawg rushed to battle,
Like the woodland boar was the gash of the hewer;
He was the bull of battle in the conflicting fight;
He allured wild dogs with his hand.
My witnesses are Owain the son of Eulad,
And Gwryen, and Gwyn, and Gwryad.
From Catraeth, from the conflict,
From Bryn Hydwn, before it was taken,
After having clear mead in his hand,

Gwrien did not see his father.

XXXI

The men marched with speed, together they bounded onward;
Short–lived were they—having become drunk over the clarified mead.
The retinue of Mynyddawg, renowned in a trial,
Their life was the price of their banquet of mead;—
Caradawg and Madawg, Pyll and Ieuan,
Gwgawn and Gwiawn, Gwyn and Cynvan,
Peredur with steel arms, Gwawrddur and Aeddan.
A defence were they in the tumult, though with shattered shields,
When they were slain, they also slaughtered;
Not one to his native home returned.

XXXII

The men marched with speed, together were they regaled
That year over mead; great was their design:
How sad to mention them! how grievous the longing for them!
Their retreat was poison; no mother's son nurses them.
How long the vexation and how long the regret for them—
For the brave men of the wine–fed region!
Gwlyged of Gododdin, having partaken of the inciting
Banquet of Mynyddawg, performed illustrious deeds,
And dear was the price he gave for the purchase of the conflict of Catraeth.

XXXIII

The men went to Catraeth in battle–array and with shout of war,
With the strength of steeds, and with dark–brown harness, and with shields,
With uplifted javelins, and sharp lances,
With glittering mail, and with swords.
He excelled, he penetrated through the host,
Five battalions fell before his blade;

Ruvawn Hir,—he gave gold to the altar,
And gifts and precious stones to the minstrel.

XXXIV

No hall was ever made so loquacious,—
So great, so magnificent for the slaughter.
Morien procured and spread the fire,
He would not say that Cenon would not make a corpse
Of one harnessed, armed with a pike, and of wide–spread fame.
His sword resounded on the top of the rampart.
No more than a huge stone can be removed from its fixed place
Will Gwid, the son of Peithan, be moved.

XXXV

No hall was ever so full of delegates:
Had not Moryen been like Caradawg,
With difficulty could he have escaped towards Mynawg.
Fierce, he was fiercer than the son of Fferawg;
Stout was his hand, he set flames to the retreating horsemen.
Terrible in the city was the cry of the multitude;
The van of the army of Gododdin was scattered;
In the day of wrath he was nimble—and was he not destructive in retaliating?
The dependants of Mynyddawg deserved their horns of mead.

XXXVI

No hall was ever made so immovable
As that of Cynon of the gentle breast, sovereign of valuable treasures.
He sat no longer at the upper end of the high seat.
Those whom he pierced were not pierced again;
Sharp was the point of his lance;
With his enamelled armour he penetrated through the troops;
Swift in the van were the horses, in the van they tore along.

In the day of wrath, destruction attended his blade,
When Cynon rushed forward with the green dawn.

XXXVII

A grievous descent was made on his native place;
He repelled aggression, he fixed a boundary;
His spear forcibly pushed the laughing chiefs of war:
Even as far as Effyd reached his valour, which was like that of Elphin;
Eithinyn the renowned, an ardent spirit, the bull of conflict.

XXXVIII

A grievous descent was made on his native place,
The price of mead in the hall, and the feast of wine;
His blades were scattered about between two armies,
Illustrious was the knight in front of Gododdin.
Eithinyn the renowned, an ardent spirit, the bull of conflict.

XXXIX

A grievous descent was made in front of the extended riches;
The army dispersed with trailing shields.—
A shivered shield before the herd of the roaring Beli.
A dwarf from the bloody field hastened to the fence;
On our part there came a hoary–headed man to take counsel.
On a prancing steed, bearing a message from the golden–torqued leader.
Twrch proposed a compact in front of the destructive course:
Worthy was the shout of refusal;
We cried, 'Let heaven be our protection;
Let his compact be that he should be prostrated by the spear in battle.'
The warriors of the far–famed Aclud
Would not contend without prostrating his host to the ground.

XL

For the piercing of the skilful and most learned man,
For the fair corpse which fell prostrate on the ground,
For the failing of the hair from off his head,
From the grandson of the eagle of Gwydien,
Did not Gwyddwg defend with his spear,
Resembling and honouring his master?
Morieu of the sacred song defended
The wall, and deposed the head
Of the chief in the ground, both our support and our sovereign
Equal to three men, to please the maid, was Bradwen,
Equal to twelve was Gwenabwy the son of Gwen.

XLI

For the piercing of the skilful and most learned man,
He bore a shield in the action;
With energy did the stroke of his sword fall on the head.
In Lloegyr he caused gashings before three hundred chieftains.
He who takes hold of a wolf's mane without a club
In his hand, must naturally have a brave disposition under his cloak.
In the engagement of wrath and carnage
Bradwen perished—he did not escape.

XLII

A man moved rapidly on the wall of the Caer,
He was of a warlike disposition; neither a house nor a city was actively engaged in battle.
One weak man, with his shouts,
Endeavoured to keep off the birds of battle.
Surely Syll of Mirein relates that there were more
That had chanced to come from Llwy,
From around the inlet of the flood;
Surely he relates that there were more

At an early hour,
Equal to Cynhaval in merit.

XLIII

When thou, famous conqueror!
Wast protecting the ear of corn in the uplands
Deservedly were we said to run like men of mark.
The entrance to Din Drei was not guarded.
Such as was fond of treasure took it;
There was a city for the army that should venture to enter.
Gwynwyd was not called, where he was not.

XLIV

Since there are a hundred men in one house,
I know the cares of distress.
The chief of the men must pay the contribution.

XLV

I am not headstrong and petulant.
I will not avenge myself on him who drives me.
I will not laugh in derision.
Under foot for a while,
My knee is stretched,
My hands are bound,
In the earthen house,
With an iron chain
Around my two knees.
Yet of the mead from the horn,
And of the men of Catraeth,
I, Aneurin, will compose,
As Taliesin knows,
An elaborate song,

Or a strain to Gododdin,
Before the dawn of the brightest day.

XLVI

The chief exploit of the North did the hero accomplish;
Of a generous breast was he, liberal is his progeny;
There does not walk upon the earth, mother has not borne.
Such an illustrious, powerful, iron–clad warrior.
By the force of the gleaming sword he protected me,
From the dismal earthen prison he brought me out,
From the place of death, from a hostile region:—
Ceneu, the son of Llywarch, energetic, bold.

XLVII

He would not bear the reproach of a congress,
Senyllt, with his vessels full of mead;
He enriched his sword with deeds of violence;
He enriched those who rushed to war;
And with his arm made pools (of blood).
In front of the armies of Gododdin and Brennych.
Fleet horses were customary in his hall.
There was streaming gore, and dark–brown harness.
A long stream of light there was from his hand.
And like a hunter shooting with the bow
Was Gwen; and the attacking parties mutually repulsed each other,
Friend and foe by turns;
The men did not cut their way to flee,
But they were the general defenders of every region.

XLVIII

Llech Lleutu and Tud Lleudvre,
The course of Gododdin,

The course of Ragno, close at hand,
The hand that was director of the splendour of battle,
With the branch of Caerwys.
Before it was shattered
By the season of the storm, by the storm of the season,
To form a rank in front of myriads of men,
Coming from Dindywydd,
Excited with rage,
Deeply did they design,
Sharply did they pierce,
Wholly did the host chant,
Battered was their shield;
Before the bull of conflict
Their van was broken.

XLIX

His languid foes trembled greatly,
Since the battle of most active tumult,
At the border of Banceirw,
Around the border of Bancarw;
The fingers of Brych will break the bar,
For Pwyll, for Disteir, for Distar,
For Pwyll, for Roddig, for Rychwardd,
A strong bow was spent by Rys in Riwdrech.
They that were not bold did not attain their purpose;
None escaped that was once overtaken and pierced.

L

It was no good deed that his shield should be pierced.
On the side of his horse;
Not meetly did he place his thigh
On the long–legged, slender, gray charger.
Dark was his shaft, dark,

Darker was his saddle.
Thy man is in his cell,
Gnawing the shoulder of a buck;
May he have the benefit of his hand!
Far be he!

LI

It was well that Adonwy came to Gwen;
Gwen was left without Bradwen.
Thou didst fight, kill, and burn,
Thou didst not do worse than Moryen;
Thou didst not regard the rear or the van.
Of the towering figure without a helmet.
Thou didst not observe the great swelling sea of knights.
That would hew down, and grant no quarter to the Saxons.

LII

Gododdin, in respect of thee will I demand
The dales beyond the ridges of Drum Essyd.
The slave to the love of money is without self–control.
By the counsel of thy son let thy valour shine forth.
It was not a degrading advice.
In front of Tan Veithin,
From twilight to twilight, the edge gleamed.
Glittering exterior had the purple of the pilgrim.
Gwaws, the defenceless, the delight of the bulwark of battle, was slain.
His scream was inseparable from Aneurin.

LIII

Together arise the associated warriors,
To Catraeth the loquacious multitude eagerly march;
The effect of mead in the hall, and the beverage of wine.

Blades were scattered between the two armies.
Illustrious was the knight in front of Gododdin:—
Eithinyn the renowned, an ardent spirit, the bull of conflict.

LIV

Together arise the associated warriors,
Strangers to the country, their deeds shall be heard of.
The bright wave murmured along on its pilgrimage,
While the young deer were in full melody.
Among the spears of Brych thou couldst see no rods.
Merit does not accord with the rear.
Moryal in pursuit will not countenance evil deeds,
With his steel blade ready for the effusion of blood.

LV

Together arise the associated warriors.
Strangers to the country, their deeds shall be heard of.
There was slaughtering with axes and blades,
And there was raising large cairns over the men of toil.

LVI

Together arise the warriors, together met,
And all with one accord sallied forth;
Short were their lives, long is the grief of those who loved them.
Seven times their number of Lloegrians they had slain;
After the conflict women raised a lamentation;
Many a mother has the tear on her eyelash.

LVII

No hall was ever made so faultless
Nor a hero so generous, with the aspect of a lion of the greatest course,

As Cynon of the gentle breast, the most comely lord.
The city, its fame extends to the remotest parts;
It was the staying shelter of the army, the benefit of flowing melody.
In the world, engaged in arms, the battle–cry,
And war, the most heroic was he;
He slew the mounted ravagers with the sharpest blade;
Like rushes did they fall before his hand.
Son of Clydno, of lasting fame! I will sing
To thee a song of praise without limit, without end.

LVIII

From the banquet of wine and mead
They deplored the death
Of the mother of Hwrreith.
The energetic Eidiol.
Honoured her in front of the hill,
And before Buddugre,
The hovering ravens
Ascend in the sky.
The foremost spearmen fall
Like a virgin–swarm around him
Without the semblance of a retreat
Warriors in wonder shook their javelins,
With pallid lips,
Caused by the keenness of the destructive sword.
Wakeful was the carousal at the beginning of the banquet;
To–day sleepless is
The mother of Reiddun, the leader of the tumult.

LIX

From the banquet of wine and mead
They went to the strife
Of mail–clad warriors: I know no tale of slaughter which accords

So complete a destruction as has happened.
Before Catraeth, loquacious was the host.
Of the retinue of Mynyddawg, the unfortunate hero,
Out of three hundred but one man returned.

LX

From the banquet of wine and mead they hastened,
Men renowned in difficulty, careless of their lives;
In bright array around the viands they feasted together;
Wine and mead and meal they enjoyed.
From the retinue of Mynyddawg I am being ruined;
And I have lost a leader from among my true friends.
Of the body of three hundred men that hastened to
Catraeth, alas! none have returned but one alone.

LXI

Pressent, in the combat of spears, was impetuous as a ball,
And on his horse would he be, when not at home;
Yet illusive was his aid against Gododdin.
Of wine and mead he was lavish;
He perished on the course;
And under red−stained warriors
Are the steeds of the knight, who in the morning had been bold.

LXII

Angor, thou who scatterest the brave,
Like a serpent thou piercest the sullen ones,
Thou tramplest upon those that are clad in strong mail
In front of the army:
Like an enraged bear, guarding and assaulting,
Thou tramplest upon spears.
In the day of conflicts

In the swampy entrenchment:
Like Neddig Nar,
Who in his fury prepared
A feast for the birds,
In the tumultuous fight.
Upright thou art called from thy righteous deed,
Before the director and bulwark of the course of war,
Merin, and Madyen, it is fortunate that thou wert born.

LXIII

It is incumbent to sing of the complete acquisition
Of the warriors, who around Catraeth made a tumultuous rout.
With confusion and blood, treading and trampling.
The strength of the drinking horn was trodden down, because it had held mead;
And as to the carnage of the interposers
Cibno does not relate, after the commencement of the action.
Since thou hast received the communion thou shalt be interred.

LXIV

It is incumbent to sing of so much renown,
The loud noise of fire, and of thunder, and of tempest,
The noble manliness of the knight of conflict.
The ruddy reapers of war are thy desire,
Thou man of might! but the worthless wilt thou behead,
In battle the extent of the land shall hear of thee.
With thy shield upon thy shoulder thou dost incessantly cleave
With thy blade (until blood flows) like refined wine from glass vessels.
As money for drink, thou art entitled to gold.
Wine–nourished was Gwaednerth, the son of Llywri.

LXV

It is incumbent to sing of the illustrious retinue,
That, after the fatal impulse, filled Aeron.
Their hands satisfied the mouths of the brown eagles,
And prepared food for the beasts of prey.
Of those who went to Catraeth, wearing the golden torques,
Upon the message of Mynyddawg, sovereign of the people,
There came not without reproach on behalf of the Brython,
To Gododdin, a man from afar better than Cynon.

LXVI

It is incumbent to sing of so skilful a man;
joyous was he in the hall; his life was not without ambition;
Bold, all around the world would Eidol seek for melody;
For gold, and fine horses., and intoxicating mead.
Only one man of those who loved the world returned,—
Cynddilig of Aeron, the grandson of Enovant.

LXVII

It is incumbent to sing of the illustrious retinue
That went on the message of Mynyddawg, sovereign of the people,
And the daughter of Eudav Hir, the scourge of Gwananhon,
Who was appareled in purple robes, certain to cause manglings.

LXVIII

The warriors celebrated the praise of Nyved,
When in their presence fire was lighted.
On Tuesday, they put on their dark–brown garments;
On Wednesday, they polished their enamelled armour;
On Thursday, their destruction was certain;
On Friday, was brought carnage all around:

On Saturday, their joint I a hour did no execution;
On Sunday, their blades assumed a ruddy hue;
On Monday, was seen a pool knee–deep of blood.
Truly, the Gododdin relates that, after the toil,
Before the tents of Madawg, when he returned,
Only one man in a hundred came back.

LXIX

Early rising in the morn
There was a conflict at the Aber in front of the course,
The pass and the knoll were in conflagration.
Like a boar didst thou lead to the mount,
There was treasure for him that was fond of it; there was room;
And there was the blood of dark–brown hawks.

LXX

Early rising in an instant of time,
After kindling a fire at the Aber in front of the fence,
After leading his men in close array,
In front of a hundred he pierced the foremost.
It was sad that you should have caused a gushing of blood,
Like the drinking of mead in the midst of laughter.
It was brave of you to stay the little man
With the fierce and impetuous stroke of the sword.
How irresistible was he when he would kill
The foe! would that his equal could be found!

LXXI

He fell headlong down the precipice;
Song did not support his noble head:
It was a violation of privilege to kill him when bearing the branch,
It was the usage that Owain should ascend upon the course,

And extend, before the onset, the best branch,
And that he should pursue the study of meet and learned strains.
An excellent man was he, the assuager of tumult and battle,
His grasp dreaded a sword;
In his hand he bore an empty corselet.
O sovereign, dispense rewards
Out of his precious shrine.
Eidol, with frigid blood and pallid countenance,
Spreading carnage, his judgment was just and supreme,
Owner of horses
And strong trappings,
And ice–like shields;
Instantaneously he makes an onset, ascending and descending.]

LXXII

The leader of war with eagerness conducts the battle,
A mighty country loves mighty reapers.
Blood is a heavy return for new mead.
His cheeks are covered with armour all around,
There is a trampling of accoutrements—accoutrements are trampled.
He calls for death and brings desolation.
In the first onset his lances penetrate the targets,
And for light on the course, shrubs blaze on the spears.

LXXIII

A conflict on all sides destroyed thy cell;
And a hall there was to thee, where used to be poured out
Mead, sweet and ensnaring.
Gwrys make the battle clash with the dawn;
The fair gift of the tribes of the Lloegrians;
Punishment he inflicted until a reverse came.
May the dependants of Gwynedd hear of his renown.
Gwananhon will be his grave.

The lance of the conflict of Gwynedd,
The bull of the host, the oppressor of sovereigns,
Before earth pressed upon him, before he lay down;
Be the extreme boundary of Gododdin his grave!

LXXIV

An army is accustomed to be in hardships.
Mynawg, the bitter-handed leader of the forces,
He was wise, ardent, and stately:
At the social banquet he was not at all harsh.
They removed the valuable treasures that were in his possession:
And not the image of anything for the benefit of the region was left.
We are called! Like the sea is the tumult in the conflict;
Spears are mutually darting—spears all equally destructive;
Impelled are sharp weapons of iron, gashing even the ground,
And with a clang the sock falls on the pate.
A successful warrior was Fflamddur against the enemy.

LXXV

He supported war-horses and war-harness.
Drenched with gore on red-stained Catraeth
Is the shaft of the army of Dinus,
The angry dog of war upon the towering hill.
We are called to the honourable post of assault;
Most conspicuous is the iron-clad Heiddyn.

LXXVI

Mynawg of the impregnable strand of Gododdin,
Mynawg, for him our cheeks are sad:
Before the raging flame of Eiddyn he turned not aside.
He stationed men of firmness at the entrance,
He placed a thick covering in the van,

Vigorously he descended upon the furious foe;
He caused devastation and sustained great weight.
Of the retinue of Mynyddawg there escaped none
Except one frail weapon, tottering every way.

LXXVII

Since the loss of Moryed there was no shield–bearer,
To support the strand, or to set the ground on fire;
Firmly did he grasp in his hand a blue blade,
A shaft ponderous as a chief priest's crozier;
He rode a gray stately–headed courser,
And behind his blade there was a dreadful fall of slaughter;
When overpowered, he did not run away from the battle.
He poured out to us sparkling mead, sweet and ensnaring.

LXXVIII

I beheld the array from the high land of Adoyn;
They descended with the sacrifice for the conflagration;
I saw what was usual, a continual running to the town,
And the men of Nwythyon entirely lost;
I saw men in complete order approaching with a shout;
And the heads of Dyvynwal and Breych, ravens devoured them.

LXXIX

Blessed conqueror, of temper mild, the bone of the people,
With his blue streamer displayed, while the foes range the sea.
Brave is he on the waters, most numerous his host;
With a bold breast and loud shout they pierced him.
It was his custom to make a descent before nine armaments,
In the face of blood, of the country, and of the tribes.
I love the victor's throne which was for harmonious strains,
Cynddilig of Aeron, the lion's whelp!

LXXX

I could wish to have been the first to fall in Catraeth,
As the price of mead in the hall, and the beverage of wine;
I could wish to have been pierced by the blade,
Ere he was slain on the green plain of Uffin.
I loved the son of renown, who caused blood to flow,
And made his sword descend upon the violent.
Can a tale of valour before Gododdin be related,
In which the son of Ceidiaw has not his fame as a man of war?

LXXXI

It is sad for me, after our toil,
To suffer the pang of death through indiscretion;
And doubly grievous and sad for me to see
Our men falling from head to foot,
With a long sigh and with reproaches.
After the strenuous warriors of our native land and country,
Ruvawn and Gwgawn, Gwiawn and Gwlyged,
Men most gallant at their posts, valiant in difficulties,
May their souls, now after the conflict,
Be received into the country of heaven, the abode of tranquillity.

LXXXII

He repelled the chain through a pool of blood,
He slaughtered like a hero such as asked no quarter.
With a sling and a spear; he flung off his glass goblet
Of mead; in the presence of sovereigns he overthrew an army.
His counsel prevailed wherever he spoke.
A multitude that had no pity would not be allowed
Before the onset of his battle−axes and sword;
Sharpened they were; and his sounding blade was carefully watched.

LXXXIII

A supply of an army,
A supply of lances,
And a host in the vanguard,
With a menacing front:
In the day of strenuous exertion,
In the eager conflict,
They displayed their valour.
After intoxication,
And the drinking of mead,
There was no deliverance.
They watched us
For a while;
When it shall be related how the attack
Of horses and men was repelled, it will be pronounced the decree of fate.

LXXXIV

Why should so much anxiety come to me?
I am anxious about the maid—
The maid that is in Arddeg.
There is a precipitate running,
And lamentation along the course.
Affectionately have I deplored,
Deeply have I loved,
The illustrious dweller of the wood!
And the men of Argoed.
Woe to those who are accustomed
To be marshalled for battle!
He pressed hard upon the hostile force, for the benefit of chieftains,
Through rough woods,
And dammed–up waters,
To the festivities,
At which they caroused together: he conducted us to a bright fire,

And to a white and fresh hide.
Gereint from the south raised a shout;
A brilliant gleam reflected on the pierced shield.
Of the lord of the spear, a gentle lord;
Attached to the glory of the sea.
Posterity will accomplish
What Gereint would have done.
Generous and resolute wert thou!

LXXXV

Instantaneously his fame is wafted on high,
Irresistible was Angor in the conflict,
Unflinching eagle of the forward heroes;
He bore the toil, brilliant was his zeal;
He outstripped fleetest horses in war;
But he was mild when the wine from the goblet flowed.
Before the new mead, and his cheek became pale,
He was a man of the banquet over delicious mead from the bowl.

LXXXVI

With slaughter was every region filled;
His courage was like a fetter:
The front of his shield was pierced.
Disagreeable is the delay of the wrathful
To defend Rywoniawg.
The second time they raised the shout, and were crushed
By the war–horses with gory trappings.
An immovable army will his warlike nobles form,
And the field was reddened when he was greatly enraged.
Severe in the conflict, with a blade he slaughtered;
Sad news from the battle he brought;
And a New–year's song he composed.
Adan, the son of Ervai, there was pierced,

Adan! the haughty boar, was pierced,
One damsel, a maid, and a hero.
And when he was only a youth he had the rights of a king.
Being lord of Gwyndyd, of the blood of Glyd Gwaredawg.
Ere the turf was laid on the gentle face
Of the generous dead, now undisturbed,
He was celebrated for fame and generosity.
This is the grave of Garthwys Hir from the land of Rywoniawg.

LXXXVII

The coat of Dinogad was of various colours,
And made of the speckled skins of young wolves.
'Whistle! whistle!' the juggling sound!
I fain would dispraise it; it is dispraised by eight slaves.
When thy father went out to hunt,
With his pole on his shoulder, and his provisions in his hand,
He would call to his dogs of equal size,—
'Catch it! catch it! seize it! seize it!'
He would kill a fish in his coracle,
As a noble lion kills (his prey).
When thy father went up to the mountain
He would bring back the head of a roebuck, the head of a wild boar, the head of a stag,
The head of a spotted moor–hen from the mountain,
The head of a fish from the falls of Derwennyd.
As many as thy father could reach with his flesh–hook,
Of wild boars, lions, and foxes.
None would escape except those that were too nimble.

LXXXVIII

If distress were to happen to me through extortion,
There would not come, there would not be to me anything more calamitous.
No man has been nursed in a hall who could be braver
Than he, or steadier in battle.

And on the ford of Penclwyd his horses were the best;
Far–spread was his fame, compact his armour;
And before the long grass covered him beneath the sod,
He, the only son of Ffervarch, poured out the horns of mead.

LXXXIX

I saw the array from the headland of Adoyn,
Carrying the sacrifice to the conflagration;
I saw the two who from their station quickly fell;
By the commands of Nwython greatly were they afflicted.
I saw the men, who made a great breach, with the dawn at Adoyn;
And the head of Dyvynwal Vych, ravens devoured it.

XC

Gododdin, in respect of thee will I demand
In the presence of a hundred that are named with deeds of valour.
And of Gwarchan, the son of Dwywei of gallant bravery,
Let it be forcibly seized in one region.
Since the stabbing of the delight of the bulwark of battle,
Since earth has gone upon Aneurin,
My cry has not been separated from Gododdin.

XCI

Echo speaks of the formidable and dragon–like weapons,
And of the fair game which was played in front of the unclaimed course of Gododdin.
He brought a supply of wine into the tents of the natives,
In the season of the storm, when there were vessels on the sea,
When there was a host on the sea, a well–nourished host.
A splendid troop of warriors, successful against a myriad of men,
Is coming from Dindywydd n Dyvnwydd.
Before Doleu in battle, worn out were their shields, and battered their helmets.

XCII

With slaughter was every region filled.
His courage was like a fetter;
The front of his shield was pierced.
Disagreeable is the delay of the brave
To defend Rywyniawg.
The second time they reposed, and were crushed
By the war–horses with gory trappings.
An immovable army will his warlike and brave nobles form,
When they are greatly affronted.
Severe in the conflict with blades he slaughtered;
Sad news from the battle he brought;
And an hundred New–years' songs he composed.
Adan, the son of Urvai, was pierced;
Adan, the haughty boar, was pierced;
One damsel, a maid, and a hero.
And when he was only a youth he had the rights of a king,
Lord of Gwyndyd, of the blood of Cilydd Gwaredawg
Ere the turf was laid on the face of the generous dead,
Wisely collected were his treasure, praise, and high–sounding fame.
The grave of Gorthyn Hir from the highlands of Rywynawg.

XCIII

For the piercing of the skilful and most learned man,
For the fair corpse which fell prostrate on the ground,
Thrice six persons judged the atrocious deed early in the morning;
And Morien lifted up his ancient lance,
And, shouting, unbent his tight–drawn bow
Towards the Gwyr, and the Gwyddyl, and Prydein.
Towards the lovely, slender, bloodstained body
The sigh of Gwenabwy, the son of Gwen.

XCIV

For the afflicting of the skilful and most learned man,
There was grief and sorrow, when he fell prostrate on the ground;
His banner showed his rank, and was borne by a man at his side.
A tumultuous scene was beheld in Eiddyn, and on the battle–field.
The grasp of his hand prevailed
Over the Gynt, and the Gwyddyl, and Pryden,
He who meddles with the mane of a wolf without a club in his hand,
He must naturally have a brave disposition under his cloak.
The sigh of Gwenabwy, the son of Gwen.

Printed in the United States
68480LVS00005B/61